Contents

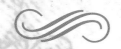

Leonardo da Vinci

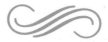

Leonardo da Vinci lived in Italy over 500 years ago. It was an exciting time for artists in Europe. Lots of rich people paid artists to make paintings and other works of art for their homes.

Leonardo was born in a village called Vinci. He was very good at science and mathematics. He wanted to find out how things worked, such as why we have thunder and lightning, how the human body works and how birds fly.

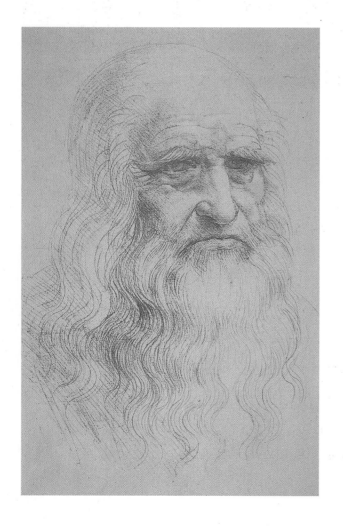

◁ *Leonardo painted this self-portrait when he was about 60 years old.*

DATES

1452 Birth of Leonardo da Vinci in Italy

1502 Leonardo paints the *Mona Lisa*

1519 Death of Leonardo da Vinci in France

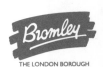
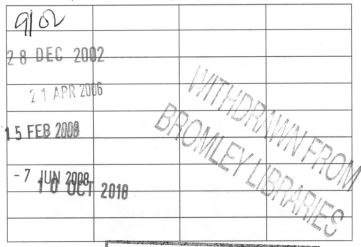

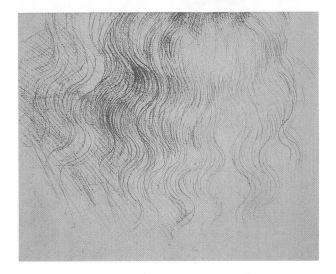

an imprint of Hodder Children's Books

FAMOUS LIVES

Kings and Queens
Saints
Inventors
Explorers
Artists
Engineers
Writers
Campaigners for Change

Series Editor: Alex Woolf
Editor: Liz Harman
Designer: Joyce Chester
Consultant: Norah Granger

First published in Great Britain in 1997 by
Wayland (Publishers) Ltd
Reprinted in 2000 by Hodder Wayland,
an imprint of Hodder Children's Books

© Hodder Wayland 1997

Hodder Children's Books, a division of Hodder Headline,
338 Euston Road, London NW1 3BH

British Library Cataloguing in Publication Data
Powell, Jillian
    Artists. – (Famous lives)
    1. Painters – Biography – Juvenile literature
    2. Painting – Juvenile literature
    I. Title
    759

ISBN 0 7502 2598 X

Typeset by Joyce Chester
Printed by EUROGRAFICA, Marano, Italy

Picture Acknowledgements
The publishers would like to thank the following for allowing their pictures to be used in this book: Abbot Hall Art Gallery & Museum, Kendal 12; © AKG, London/Rizzo 27 and 29 (bottom right); British Museum 14; Collection/Bridgeman Art Library, London 24; Collection of the Earl of Pembroke, Wilton House/Bridgeman Art Library, London 9; London, National Gallery © AKG London/Erich Lessing 15; Milan, Convent S.Marie delle Grazie, Refectory © AKG London 5; Mauritshuis, The Hague/Bridgeman Art Library, London cover (bottom left); New York, Museum of Modern Art © AKG London 26; Paris, Musee d'Orsay © AKG London/Erich Lessing 18 (top), 22; Philadeplhia Museum of Art, Pennsylvania/Bridgeman Art Library, London cover (right); Prado, Madrid/Bridgeman Art Library, London 25; Rijksmuseum, Amsterdam © AKG London 11; Science Museum cover (background) and 2–3, 7; St. Petersberg, State Ermitage © AKG London 10; Tate Gallery, London/Bridgeman Art Library, London 28 (bottom); Tate Gallery Publications 13; Turin, Biblioteca Reale © AKG London title page and 4 and 28 (top); Van Gogh Museum, Amsterdam cover (top left); Vienna, Kunsthistorisches Museum © AKG London 8 and 28 (middle); Visual Arts Library 6, 16, 17, 18 (bottom) and 29 (top), 19, 20, 21, 23 (both) and 29 (bottom left)

The following works are reproduced by permission of the copyright holders: © Succession Picasso/DACS 1996:– Pablo Picasso *Self Portrait* (1906) cover (right), Pablo Picasso *Girl With a Dove* (1901) p.24, Pablo Picasso *Woman Crying* (1937) p.25, Pablo Picasso *The Three Musicians* (1921) p. 26, photograph of Pablo Picasso with his model of a goat (1955) p. 27.

When he was about 15 years old, Leonardo went to a city called Florence to learn to be an artist. Boys like Leonardo learned art by helping in the workshops of older painters.

Leonardo's first job was to work for the Duke of the city of Milan. He planned parties and shows, played music and made drawings of buildings and weapons.

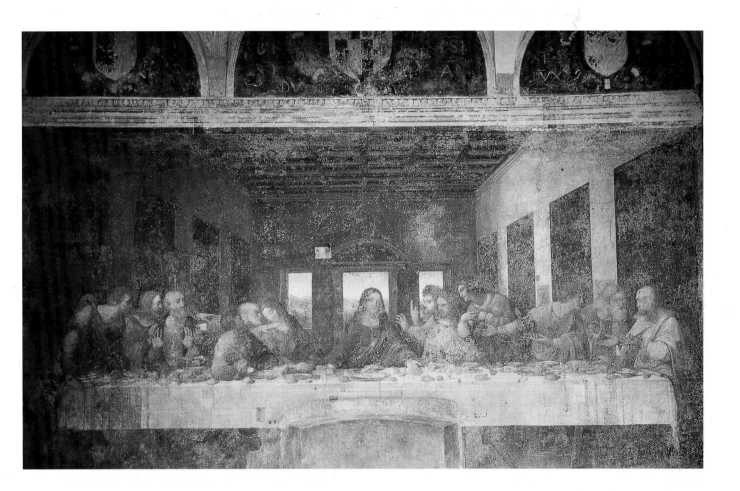

△ *While he was in Milan, Leonardo did this painting, called* The Last Supper. *He painted it on the dining-room wall of a monastery. The picture shows Christ and his disciples eating their last meal together.*

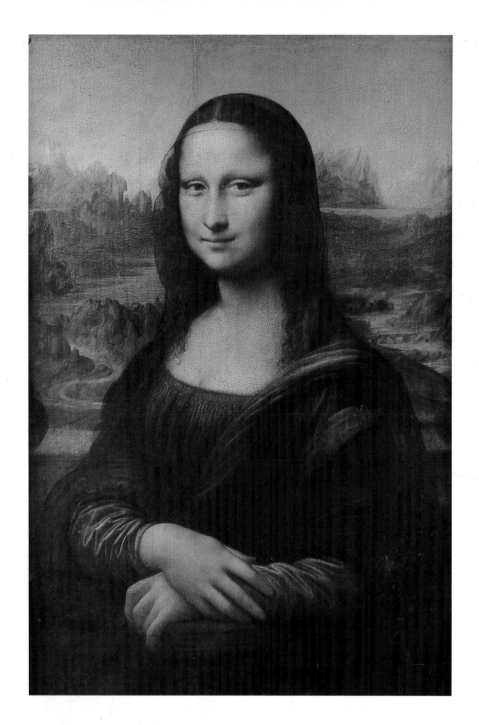

The Mona Lisa. *Leonardo painted this picture very softly. Sometimes he used his fingers to smooth the colours. He liked the painting so much that he kept it.*

When the French king took over Milan, Leonardo went back to Florence. He painted a picture called the *Mona Lisa*, which is very famous. While Leonardo painted Mona Lisa, musicians played to keep her happy. She is famous for her smile. We do not know who Mona Lisa was, but she was probably the wife of an important man.

Leonardo loved drawing and building things. He filled his notebooks with drawings of the things he saw and the ideas he had. Leonardo used a secret handwriting for his notebooks. It can only be read by looking at it in a mirror.

When Leonardo was an old man, he moved to France. He worked for the French king, Francis I. He made all sorts of machines, like a kind of bicycle and a mechanical lion.

Today, Leonardo's paintings are very famous and valuable.

Leonardo was always trying to find a way for people to fly like birds. He designed a flying machine hundreds of years before the first aeroplane was built. This drawing shows the wing. ▷

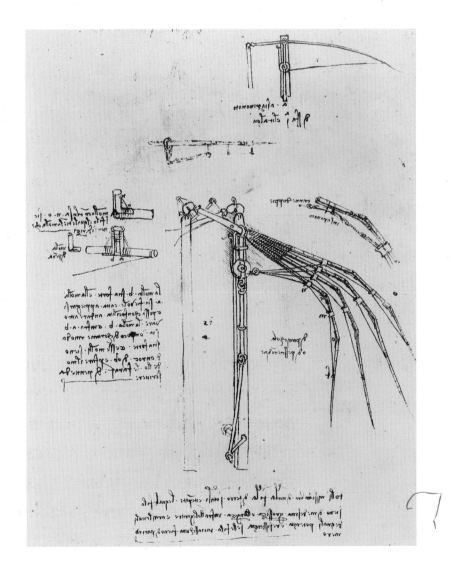

Rembrandt van Rijn

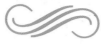

Rembrandt lived in Holland in the seventeenth century. Three hundred years ago, Holland was a very rich country. Ships from Dutch sea ports sailed all over the world and brought back goods to sell in Europe.

Rich people wanted paintings to hang in their homes. They liked pictures of themselves, country scenes and pictures of stories from the Bible or from history.

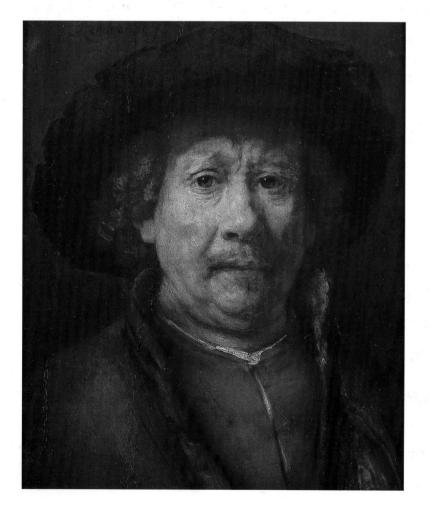

◁ All through his life, Rembrandt painted pictures of himself. He looked in a mirror and tried to show different feelings. He painted this self-portrait when he was an old man.

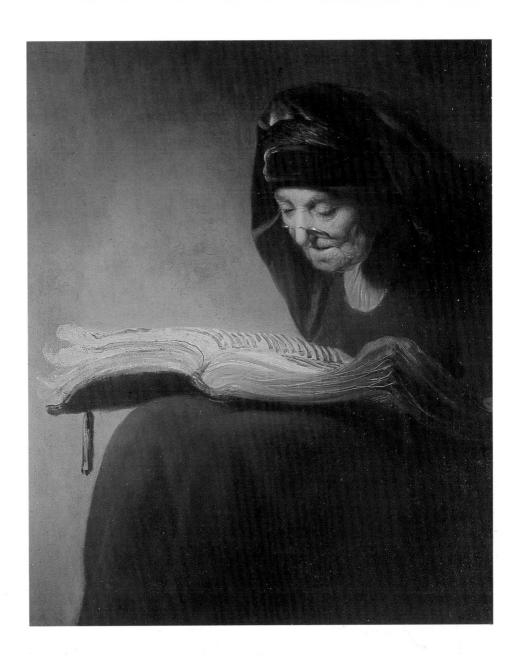

Rembrandt painted this picture of his mother. ▷

Rembrandt learned to paint in the city of Amsterdam. Then he set up a studio in his home town of Leiden. He painted pictures in oil paints, and used pen and ink for drawings. He also made tiny etchings, which are a kind of print.

Rembrandt drew people he saw in the streets. He asked his family and neighbours to dress up in costumes so that he could paint them as people from the Bible or from history.

Rembrandt returned to Amsterdam in 1631.
He married and moved into a big house with his
wife, Saskia.

Rembrandt painted lots of pictures of Saskia.
He kept a dressing-up box of costumes and
jewellery for her to wear when he painted her.

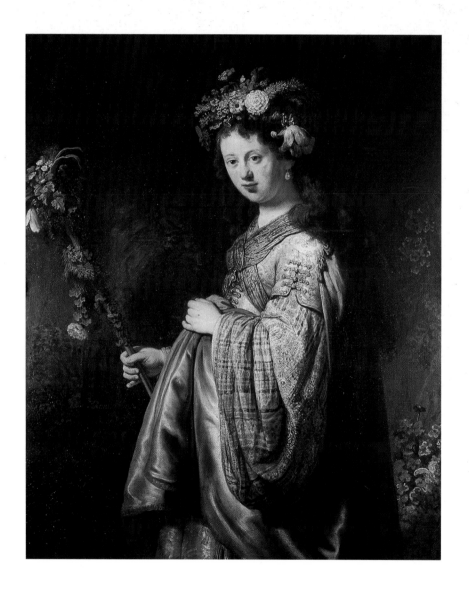

◁ *In this painting,
Rembrandt's wife Saskia
is dressed as the Roman
goddess of Spring.*

DATES

1606 Birth of
Rembrandt van Rijn
in Holland
1631 Rembrandt
moves to Amsterdam
1669 Death of
Rembrandt van Rijn

Rich people in Amsterdam paid Rembrandt to
paint their portraits. Sometimes he was asked to
paint groups of people who worked together, like
soldiers or doctors.

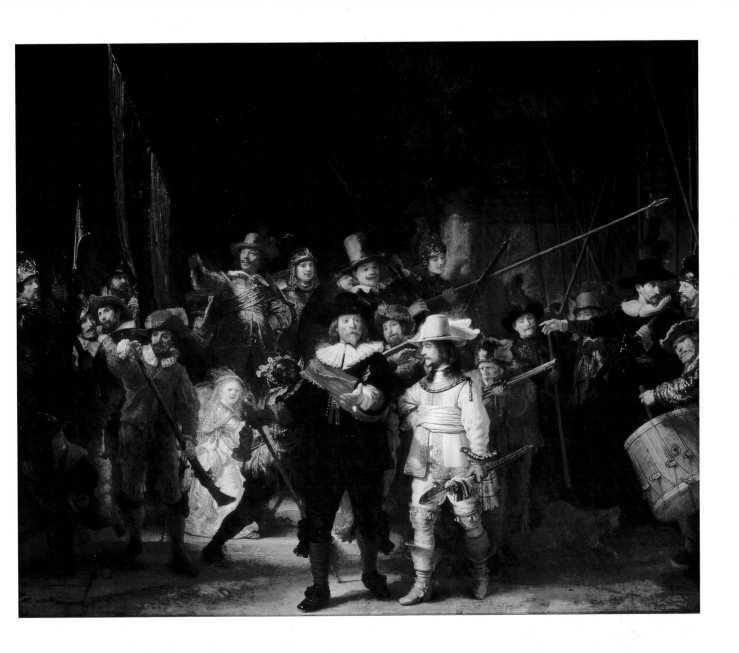

△ *Rembrandt painted this huge picture of a company of soldiers. There is a little girl in the crowd, and a dog is barking at the drummer.*

Saskia died in 1642. In the years that followed, Rembrandt spent all his money and had to move out of his house. He was a sad man, but he went on painting until he died at the age of 63.

Joseph Mallord William Turner

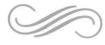

Joseph Turner grew up in London, where his
father had a barber's shop. As a boy, Turner
coloured prints for sale in the shop.

In 1789, when he was 14 years old, Turner went
to the Royal Academy art school. In the
evenings, he copied watercolour paintings to
earn some money.

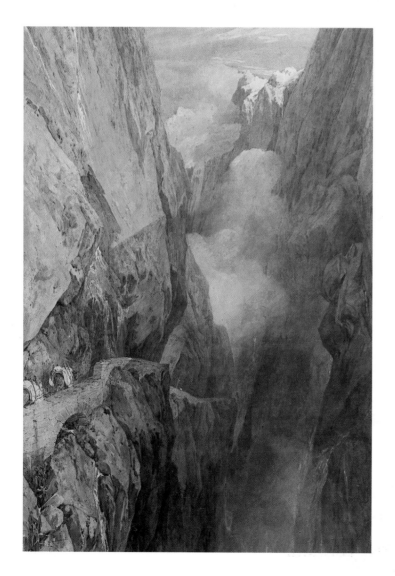

◁ *Turner painted
this picture of a
mountain pass
in Switzerland
in 1804.*

Turner was soon made a member of the Royal Academy. Only the best artists were members. Members were allowed to show their paintings in the Academy galleries.

Turner took his sketchbook with him wherever he went. He made sketches in pencil and in watercolour. He was always looking for new subjects to paint and draw.

Turner visited France and Switzerland. He copied lots of French paintings and made watercolour drawings of the mountains.

When he came back to London, Turner painted a picture of Hannibal. Hannibal was a famous soldier, who lived hundreds of years ago and crossed some mountains called the Alps.

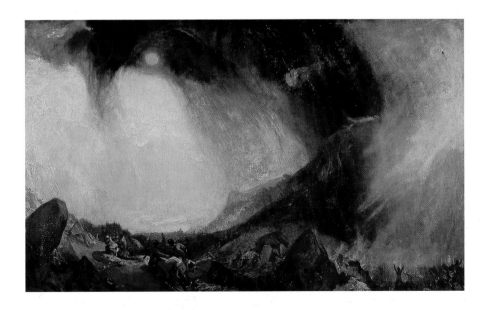

△ *Turner made up this picture from stories about Hannibal. He painted the mountains from sketches he made in Switzerland.*

Turner's next visit was to Italy. He loved the warm sunshine there. It made all the colours look so bright. He painted lots of watercolours.

Turner liked painting different kinds of weather – sun, rain, wind and snow. He once asked sailors to tie him to a ship's mast for four hours so that he could watch a really bad snowstorm!

In his paintings, Turner used lots of colours in swirling brushstrokes. He thought that colour could show happiness or sadness.

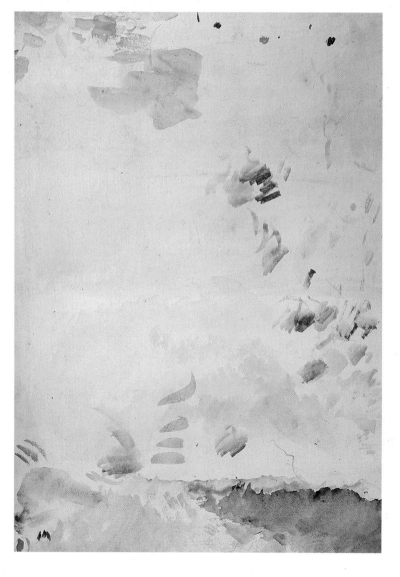

◁ *Some of the paintings Turner did in Italy are just splashes of colour, like this one.*

DATES

1775 Birth of Joseph Mallord William Turner in London
1802 Turner is made a member of the Royal Academy
1851 Death of Joseph Mallord William Turner

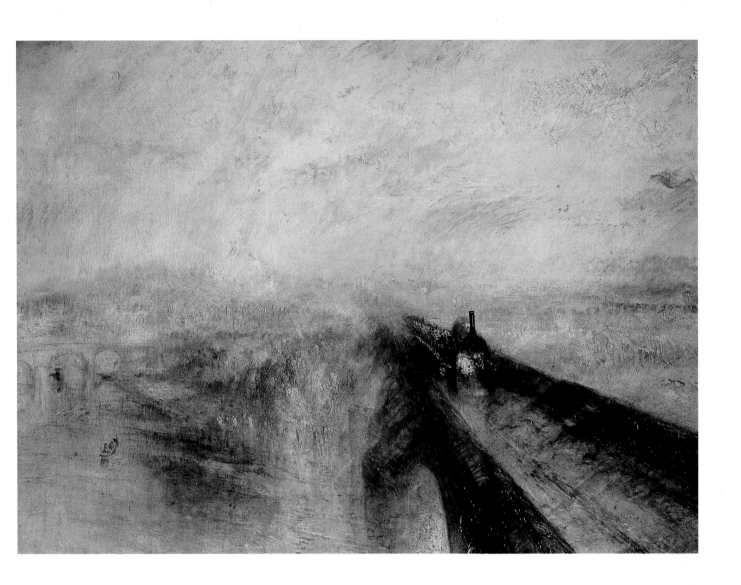

△ *Turner was very excited by the railway trains and steam ships that had just been invented. This painting of a steam train is called* Rain, Steam, Speed.

People thought Turner was very clever but they thought his paintings looked strange. Sometimes, he would add to his paintings or make changes to them when they were hanging on the walls at the art exhibition.

During his life, Turner painted nearly 300 oil paintings and 20,000 watercolours and drawings.

Vincent van Gogh

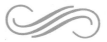

Today, Vincent van Gogh's paintings are very famous and valuable, but when he was alive, Van Gogh sold hardly any of his paintings. He was poor and unhappy for most of his short life.

Van Gogh was born in Holland about 150 years ago. As a boy, he loved looking at paintings and often visited museums and art galleries.

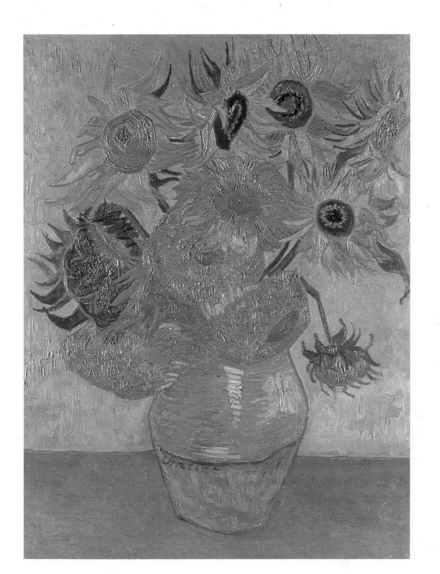

◁ Sunflowers, *painted by Van Gogh in 1888.*

DATES

1853 Birth of Vincent van Gogh in Holland
1888 Van Gogh moves to Arles in the south of France
1891 Death of Vincent van Gogh in France

This is Van Gogh's painting of a wheat field near Paris in summer. ▷

Van Gogh began to train to be a preacher, like his father. He went to Belgium and, while he was there, he taught himself to draw and paint.

Van Gogh decided that he wanted to become a painter. He went to live in Paris, where his brother, Theo, bought and sold paintings.

Van Gogh painted with bright colours, often using little dots and dashes of colour. He painted his friends, the Paris cafés and the countryside.

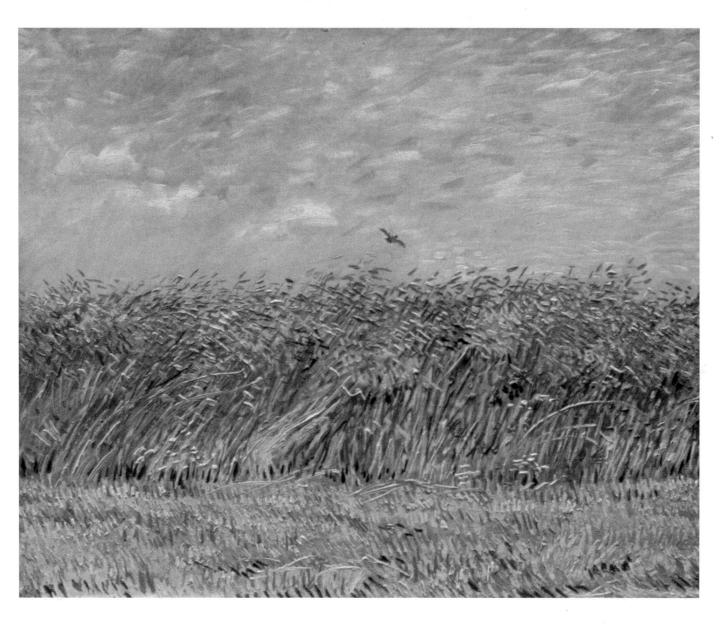

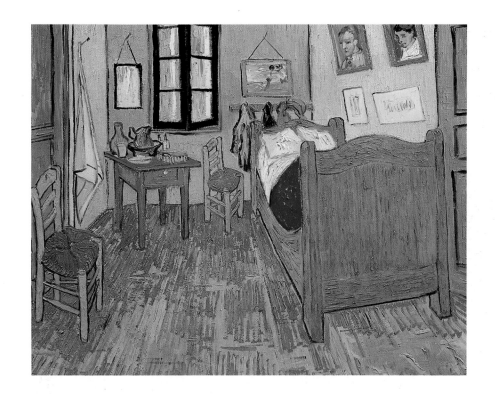

◁ Van Gogh painted this picture of his bedroom in the south of France.

In 1888, Van Gogh went to live in the south of France. He loved the sunshine there. He spent all his time painting. He used bright colours with thick paint and bold brushstrokes.

Paul Gauguin, a painter, came to stay with Van Gogh. They quarrelled and Van Gogh was so upset that he cut off part of his own ear.

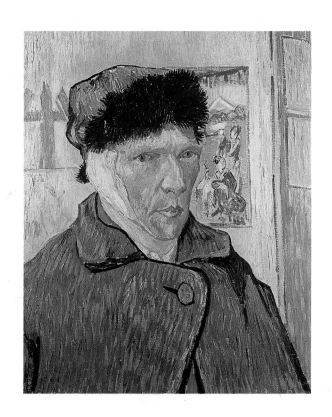

After arguing with Gauguin, Van Gogh painted this picture of himself with his cut ear bandaged. ▷

After this, Van Gogh became unwell. He went to stay in a hospital at St. Rémy. He often took his paints outdoors and painted in the fields, even at night by starlight. He was very unhappy.

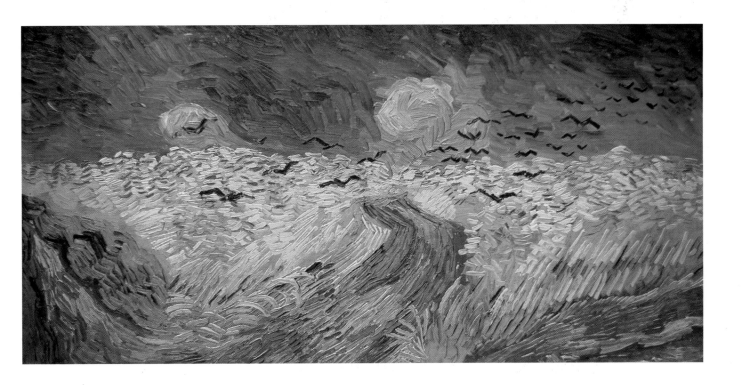

△ *This is the last picture Van Gogh painted. The black crows and stormy sky show how he was feeling.*

When he left the hospital, Van Gogh went to live in a town near Paris. A friend who was a doctor looked after him. Van Gogh's mind was full of unhappy thoughts. One day he went out into the fields and shot himself. He died a few days later. He was only 37 years old.

Claude Monet

Claude Monet was born in France in 1840. As a boy, he met a painter called Boudin, who helped him to learn how to draw and paint.

When he was a young man, Monet moved to Paris. He made friends with other young painters like Pierre Renoir and Alfred Sisley.

Until this time, painters had usually worked indoors. Monet and his friends wanted to try new ways of painting. They painted the light and the sunshine outdoors. They used bright colours and little dots and dashes of colour. This was different from the way other painters worked.

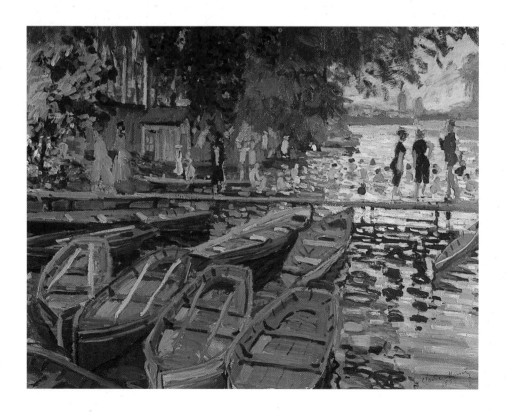

◁ *Sometimes Monet and Renoir went to paint by the River Seine in Paris. This is one of Monet's pictures of the Seine.*

People did not like these paintings. They thought the artists had not painted them properly or finished them. When Monet and his friends tried to put their paintings in exhibitions, they were rejected.

Monet and his friends decided to put on their own show. Monet put this painting in the exhibition. It is called Impression: Sunrise. *People who saw the painting started calling Monet and his friends the 'Impressionists'.* ▽

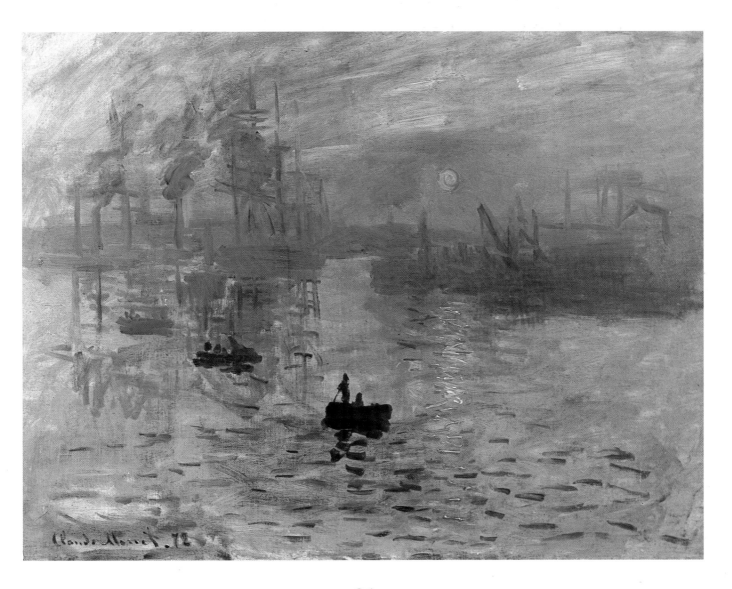

In 1883, Monet moved to a house in a country village called Giverny.

Monet went out for days in the countryside to paint. Sometimes he painted the same subject again and again. He wanted to show that the same thing can look different when the light and the weather change.

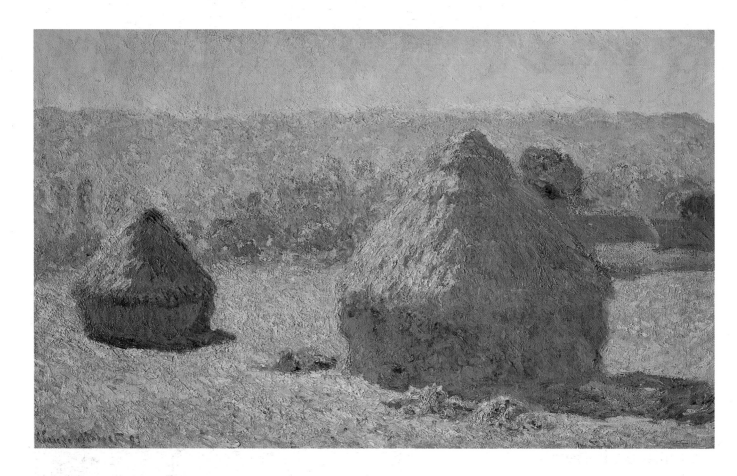

△ *Monet painted these haystacks 15 times! He liked their big round shapes and golden colour.*

Monet loved his beautiful garden at Giverny. He planted lots of trees and flowers. He made a bridge and a lily pond.

Monet went on painting when he was an old man. He died at Giverny, aged 86.

Monet painted lots of pictures of this bridge and the waterlilies in his garden. He even made huge paintings of them to go all around the walls of a room. ▷

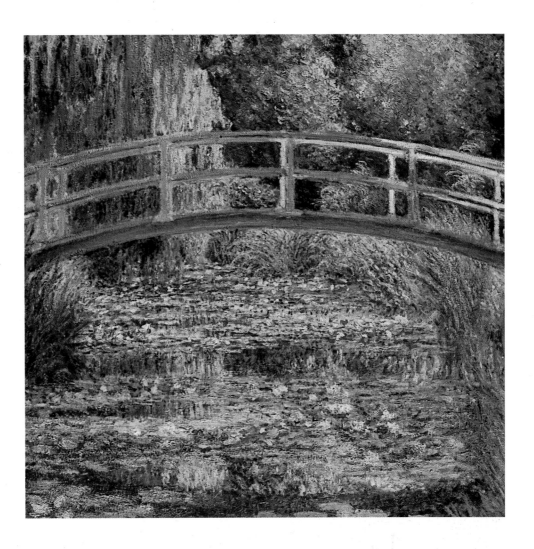

DATES

1840 Birth of Claude Monet

1874 First Impressionist exhibition is held

1926 Death of Claude Monet

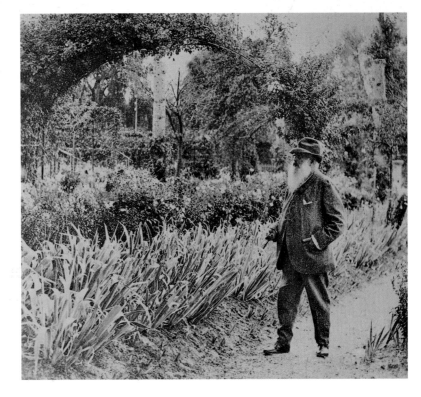

A photograph of Monet in the garden of his home at Giverny. ▷

Pablo Picasso

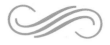

Pablo Picasso was born in 1881 in Málaga, Spain, where his father was an art teacher. Picasso went to art school to learn to paint.

When he was a young man, Picasso went to live in Paris. Artists liked living in Paris, France, where they could look at famous paintings in the art galleries and meet other painters.

Picasso was always trying different ways of painting. At first he painted sad subjects, using blue and grey paints. Then he tried painting happy pictures of actors and circus people in warm shades of pink and yellow.

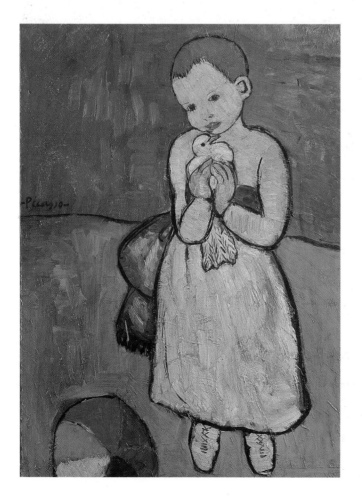

◁ *This is one of Picasso's blue paintings, showing a girl holding a dove.*

Picasso called this picture Woman Crying. *It seems as if we are looking at her from in front and from the side at the same time.* ▷

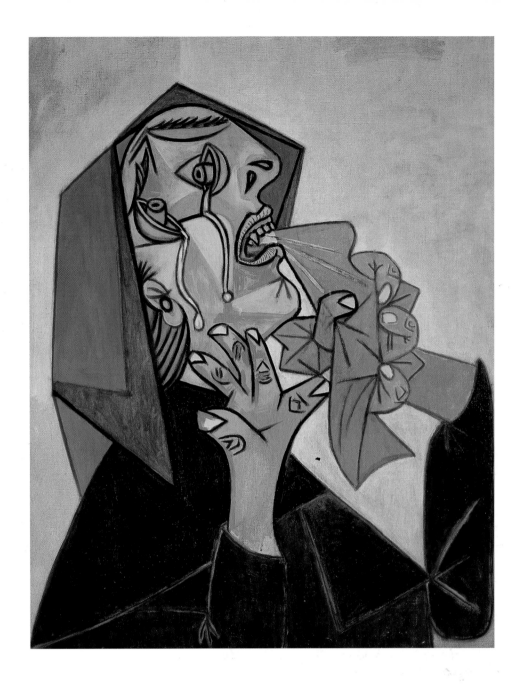

Next, Picasso tried a new way of painting.
He got the idea by looking at the bold shapes of wooden masks and figures from Africa.

Picasso worked on his new idea with his painter friend Georges Braque. They called it Cubism. They painted people and things as if they were made up of lots of different shapes, like cubes, triangles and circles.

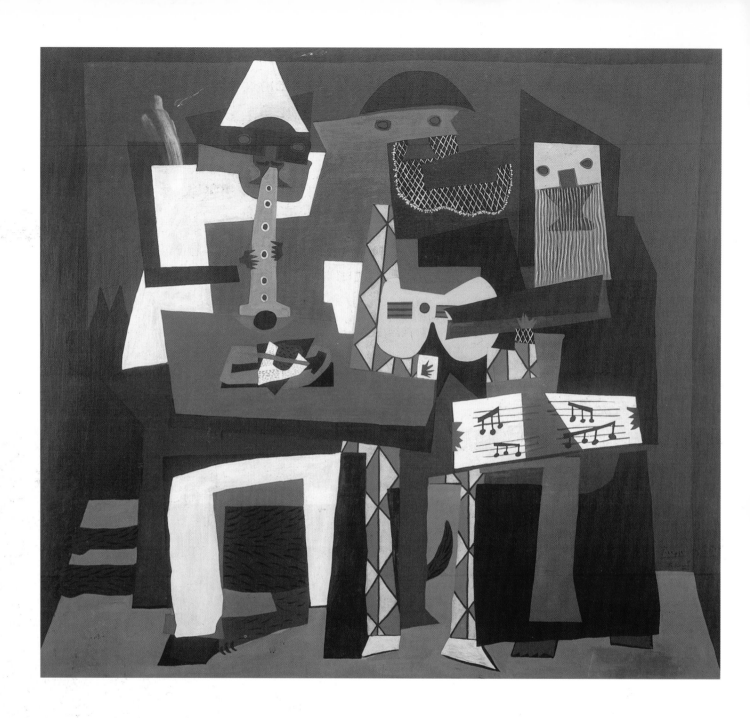

△ This is Picasso's Three Musicians, *painted in 1921.*

Sometimes Picasso made pictures by sticking pieces of paper and other materials on to board. This kind of picture is called a collage.

Picasso and Braque did not try to copy the way things really looked. They wanted to make pictures from shapes, patterns and colours. This is called Abstract art.

In the 1930s, Picasso began making models. He used pieces of junk like old bicycle wheels and handlebars. He chose shapes that he could fit together to look like something else.

Picasso carried on painting and making things until he died, aged 92. He had made many paintings, prints, models and pieces of pottery. Since his death, lots of artists have used Picasso's ideas.

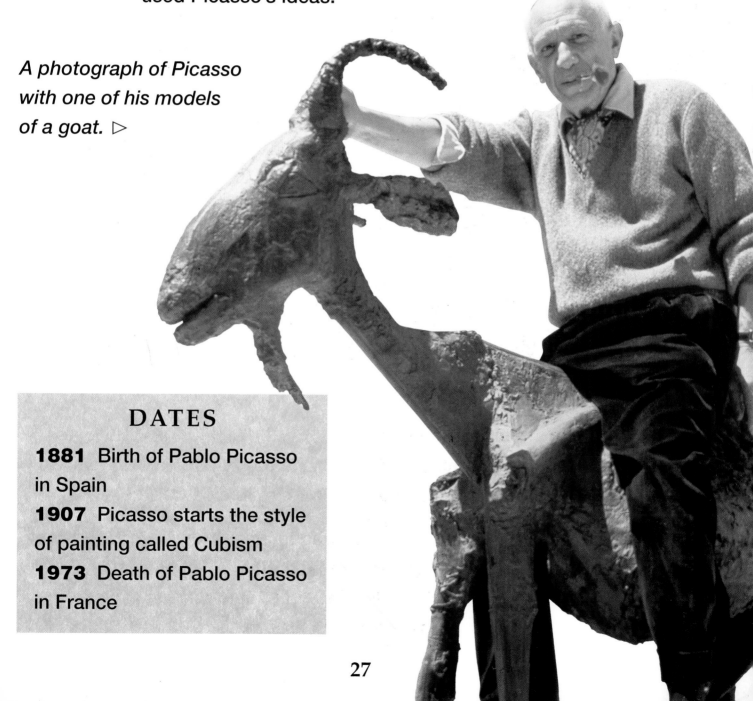

A photograph of Picasso with one of his models of a goat. ▷

DATES

1881 Birth of Pablo Picasso in Spain
1907 Picasso starts the style of painting called Cubism
1973 Death of Pablo Picasso in France

Timeline

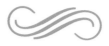

Year	Artist		How long ago?
1450			550 years ago
1452	Leonardo da Vinci born		
1499	Leonardo returns to Florence when France takes over Milan		
1500			500 years ago
1519	Death of Leonardo		
1550			450 years ago
1600			400 years ago
1606	Rembrandt van Rijn born		
1631	Rembrandt moves to Amsterdam		
1650			350 years ago
1669	Death of Rembrandt		
1700			300 years ago
1750			250 years ago
1775	Joseph Mallord William Turner born		
1800			200 years ago

Year	Artist		How long ago?
1800			200 years ago
1815	Turner paints *Hannibal Crossing the Alps*		
1840	Claude Monet born		
1850			150 years ago
1851	Death of Turner		
1853	Vincent van Gogh born		
1881	Pablo Picasso born		
1883	Monet moves to Giverny		
1889	Van Gogh cuts off part of his ear		
1891	Death of van Gogh		
1895	Picasso attends the School of Fine Arts in Barcelona		
1900			100 years ago
1926	Death of Monet		
1950			50 years ago
1973	Death of Picasso		

Words to look up

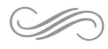

Abstract art a style of art based on colour, shape and patterns

barber's shop a place where men and boys can be shaved and have their hair cut

collage making pictures by sticking pieces of paper or other materials on to board

Cubism a style of art based on shapes like squares and triangles

disciples people who follow a person for religious reasons

etchings pictures made by printing in ink from a pattern or picture on a metal plate

exhibition a show of works of art

galleries places where works of art are on display

Impressionists a name given to artists who painted in the style used by Monet

monastery a place where monks live

oil paints paints that are mixed with oil

portraits photographs or paintings of a person

self-portrait a painting or photograph that an artist makes of themself

studio the workroom of a painter, photographer or other artist

watercolour paintings paintings that are done with watercolour paints, which are mixed with water

Other books to look at

Famous Artists series, Franklin Watts, includes titles on *Leonardo da Vinci, Monet* and *Picasso* by Antony Mason and *Van Gogh* by Andrew Hughes

Getting to Know the World's Great Artists series, Franklin Watts, includes titles on *Leonardo da Vinci, Monet, Picasso, Van Gogh* and *Rembrandt* by Mike Venezia

Introducing Picasso by Juliet Heslewood, Belitha Press, 1994

Introducing Rembrandt by Alexander Sturgis, Belitha Press, 1994

Some places to see

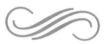

Giverny near Paris – Monet's home, where he painted many of his pictures

The Louvre in Paris, France – has paintings by Leonardo da Vinci, Monet and many other artists

Musée d'Orsay in Paris, France – has paintings by Van Gogh, Monet and many other artists

Museo Picasso in Barcelona, Spain – has many of Picasso's works

Musée Picasso in Paris, France – has many of Picasso's works

National Gallery in London – has paintings by Leonardo da Vinci, Picasso, Monet, Van Gogh, Turner and many other artists

The Rembrandthuis in Amsterdam, Holland – has many paintings by Rembrandt

Tate Gallery in London – has paintings by Turner, Van Gogh, Picasso, Monet and many others

Van Gogh Museum in Amsterdam, Holland has many paintings by Van Gogh

Index

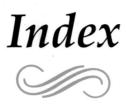